A Special Gift

for

....

with congratulations for

graduating from

....

Class of

....

Presented by

....

After the Tassel is Moved

Louis O. Caldwell

GUIDELINES FOR HIGH SCHOOL GRADUATES

Baker Books

A Division of Baker Book House Co
Grand Rapids, Michigan 49516

Published by Baker Books
a division of Baker Book House Company
P.O. Box 6287, Grand Rapids, MI 49516-6287

Printed in the United States of America

Design by Koechel Peterson & Associates, Minneapolis, MN

Library of Congress Cataloging-in-Publication Data

Caldwell, Louis O.
    After the tassel is moved : guidelines for high school graduates / Louis O. Caldwell.—2nd ed.
    p. cm.
    ISBN 0-8010-1133-7 (cloth)
    1. High school graduates—United States. 2. College choice—United States.
3. High School graduates—Employment—United States. 4. Christian life—United States.
5. Conduct of life. I. Title.
LB1695.C3 1997
248.8´3—dc20
                                           96-41988

Unless otherwise indicated, Scripture quotations are from the HOLY BIBLE, NEW INTERNATIONAL VERSION®. NIV®. Copyright © 1973, 1978, 1984 by International Bible Society. Used by permission of Zondervan Publishing House. All rights reserved.

Scripture quotations marked NKJV are from The New King James Version. Copyright © 1979, 1980, 1982, Thomas Nelson, Inc., Publishers.

The recollections of a gifted young woman (pp. 12–14) are those of Mary Libbey in the June 1963 *Reader's Digest*. Reprinted from the Fort Collins, Colorado, High School *Myriad*. Used with permission of The Reader's Digest Association, Inc.

The budget chart (p. 79) is adapted from *So You're Going to College*, published by the Sun Life Insurance Company of Canada.

To
the cherished memory
of my grandparents
Mr. and Mrs. O. W. McDonald

and

all my former students
who have experienced the thrill
of moving the tassel

Contents

Acknowledgments

My continuing gratitude to
Judi Walker,
Peggy Brown,
Nellie Gabbard,
and Shizuka Kasai,
former students of Southern Bible College,
who helped type the manuscript

To
Dr. Donald H. Bass,
a friend and colleague on the faculty of SBC,
who gave sustained support

To
Richard Baker, Dwight Baker,
Dan Van't Kerkhoff, Melinda Van Engen,
Dan Malda, and Marilyn Gordon
of Baker Book House for their hard work
in publishing this new edition

To my family:
wife, Mamie; daughter, Terri;
and sons, Louis, David, and Brad,
whose love and understanding provide
their unique encouragement

Trust in the Lord with all your heart
and lean not on your own understanding;
in all your ways acknowledge him,
and he will make your paths straight.

PROVERBS 3:5–6

That Bittersweet Moment

REMEMBER HOW IT WAS? You heard

your name called and suddenly the moment

had come. Your parents, teachers, friends, and

fellow classmates watched as you strode across

the platform to receive your diploma. Amid

the camera flashes and applause you shook

hands with your principal and accepted the

symbol of having satisfactorily completed the

equivalent of twelve years of formal education.

As you walked off the platform your next act

was deeply meaningful. You took your tassel and

moved it over to the left-hand side of your cap.
A new milestone in your life had been reached and
you knew that feeling—that bittersweet feeling—
that mixes the joys and successful struggles of the
past with the question marks and challenges of
the future.

A gifted young woman looked back from graduation and traced with insight and sensitivity the
development of an important realization: "It was
one day during the last few weeks of school," she
began, "that I first saw her. I was on my way to
the library when out of nowhere she came roller-
skating down the cracked sidewalk. As I paused
to let her go by, memories of my childhood came
surging back.

"The next day I saw her again. She was standing
across the street when school let out. After that

I saw her every day, sometimes more than once a day. She had long brown-gold curls and wore a pretty little dress that seemed strangely familiar. I never saw her face very clearly—it was always in the shadows. Who was she? Why did I see her so often? I tried to approach her, but when I came near she would run away. She would always come back though and wait somewhere in the shadows. But as graduation drew near, I had little time to wonder about that silent child who waited—for what, I didn't know.

"Commencement night came at last, with its excitement and tension, and a touch of sadness. All day long I had been rushing about, trying to keep out the memories of those past years and the friends I'd be leaving. As I went out of the house something seemed to be missing. I realized

I hadn't seen the child all day, and suddenly I felt very lonely.

"The evening passed swiftly. As we turned into the aisle to march out, I looked through the crowd, searching. There she was, sitting by my parents. As she looked at me I saw her face for the first time. In that brief moment I realized who she was and why she was there. An overwhelming sadness passed over me. This was the crossroads; she had come to say goodby."

Concluding her remarks, Mary said, "Perhaps, I would see her again, somewhere in the far distance, but it would never again be as it once had been. Our eighteen years together were ending. I had to go without her. As I went through the door, I took one last look. She was gone. I knew she would be."

Yes, Mary knew and so do you.

Nostalgic memories of those wonderful high school years blend with the realization that your achievement represents the combined efforts of a great many people. You were able to move the tassel and receive the cherished diploma because of the sacrifices and dedication of parents, teachers, counselors—everyone who contributed to your life, many of whom you will never know. Perhaps the most deeply moving of all these realizations is that of having had the unseen help of God, whose assistance has been given you in a thousand wonderful ways.

As memories linger, you can savor with deep understanding the meaning of this scriptural insight: "A longing fulfilled is sweet to the soul" (Prov. 13:19).

$\mathcal{K}$now $\mathcal{W}$here the $\mathcal{R}$ocks $\mathcal{A}$re

AFTER MOVING THE TASSEL, you can

relate to Charles F. Kettering, a successful

businessman, who said, "My interest is in the

future, because I am going to spend the rest of

my life there." An interest in the future is impor-

tant, but more is needed: Courage and direction

are also essential. Facing the uncertainty of the

future, you can identify with those who belonged

to the Hebrew nation of long ago who camped

on the brink of the Promised Land. There the

Israelites received instruction from their new

leader, Joshua, to follow the ark carried by the priests. Joshua said, "Then you will know which way to go, since you have never been this way before" (Josh. 3:4).

How modern and meaningful are the words, "since you have never been this way before." How can you know the way? After graduation, how do you know which step to take next?

Perhaps this story can help guide you. Three fishermen were anchored about a football field's distance off shore and were catching only a few fish. One of the anglers decided that he would go ashore. He stepped over the side and walked across the water to the beach. No sooner had his feet touched the sand when another of the men announced that he too would go ashore. As the third man looked on with astonishment, his buddy duplicated the performance of the first man.

"Well," thought the man who remained in the boat, "if they can do it, so can I." And over the side he went and straight to the bottom he plunged. He came splashing back to the surface and climbed back into the boat. But he was not one to give up too quickly. Again he tried but with the same results.

The two men standing on the shore had been observing the futile efforts of their friend and were so weak from laughter they could hardly stand. Finally, one managed to say to the other, "He'll drown himself if we don't hurry and tell him where the rocks are!"

So what is the wisest way to plan for your future? From this simple story, you get a clear answer: Know where the rocks are.

Your future's surface covers the "rocks," the

principles of a meaningful, effective, creative life. You do not have to have 20/20 vision to observe how often the rocks are missed. The conduct codes of today are not reliable supports or guides; cultural standards are a tide that changes and washes away faulty foundations.

Ann Landers, whose column is widely read, knows where the rocks are. She wrote: "The answer to every problem can be found between the covers of the Bible." The great Christian educator, William Lyon Phelps, professor of English at Yale, for many years used to tell his students, "I would rather have a knowledge of the Bible without a college education than a college education without a knowledge of the Bible." My own conviction as a former teacher of secondary school youth, professor of psychology for almost twenty years, and counselor for more than thirty-five years is that as you stand at your new stage in life, the Bible is your best source of help. The eternal promises and principles found in God's Word will safely guide you into your future. They will chart a course approved by God. The Creator of the terrain is best qualified to give reliable directions. The Divine Mapmaker has done his part in pointing out "where the rocks are."

So certain is Jesus Christ about the results of living life his way that he ends the greatest sermon ever taught with these words:

> "Therefore everyone who hears these words of mine and puts them into practice is like a wise man who built his house on the rock. The rain came down, the streams rose, and the winds blew and beat against that

house; yet it did not fall, because it had its foundation on the rock. But everyone who hears these words of mine and does not put them into practice is like a foolish man who built his house on sand. The rain came down, the streams rose, and the winds blew and beat against that house, and it fell with a great crash."

When Jesus had finished saying these things, the crowds were amazed at his teaching, because he taught as one who had authority, and not as their teachers of the law.

MATTHEW 7:24–29

To those who question the authority of his words, Jesus says, "My teaching is not my own. It comes from him who sent me. If anyone chooses to do God's will, he will find out whether my teaching comes from God or whether I speak on my own" (John 7:16–17).

Following the directions of the inspired Scriptures, you can be secure in the knowledge that when you take the next step into your future you will feel a rock underfoot!

Get on the Winning Side

AS THE CENTURIES HAVE PASSED,

the record of history continues to show the

incomparable commitment that Christ has

received from his followers. They have died for

him; they have lived for him. To please him was

the dominant desire of their lives. Jesus taught

his followers to pray, "Your kingdom come, your

will be done on earth as it is in heaven" (Matt.

6:10). And wherever on earth this kind of life is

being lived, there is an increase in hope, dignity,

love, justice, opportunity, and quality of life.

Unlike others who also strive for just causes, the Christian has the advantage of knowing *now* who belongs to the winning side: "At the name of Jesus every knee should bow" (Phil. 2:10); and "I am the Living One; I was dead, and behold I am alive for ever and ever" (Rev. 1:18). The open tomb and the thrilling history of the Christian church remind us of him whose way of life lives on and will ultimately triumph!

Great frontiers are yet before us. The West Coast youth who was asked about goals was wrong when he replied, "Goals? We've got no goals. Our parents have achieved them all for us." What about the physical frontier of space; the social frontier of freedom and brotherhood; the educational frontier of truth, knowledge, and understanding; and above all, the spiritual frontier of the kingdom of God?

*A*ll who involve themselves in cooperating with God in extending his kingdom find the highest purpose for living that is possible.

Cooperating Purpose

How many times have you said what is commonly known as the Lord's Prayer? Think again of the familiar words: "Your kingdom come, your will be done on earth . . ." (Matt. 6:10). These are the words Christ taught us to pray. When we repeat them in our prayers we are making a wonderful and majestic plea that his will and way of life cover the earth, that "man's inhumanity to man" cease, that peace and happiness reign everywhere, that sin and suffering be banished forever.

All who involve themselves in cooperating with God in extending his kingdom find the highest purpose for living that is possible. "The greatest use of life is to spend it for something that outlasts it," said William James. "But how," some may ask, "can I have a sense of individuality—find myself—if I live my life this way?" Christ himself gives the answer to this dilemma: "For whoever wants to save his life will lose it, but whoever loses his life for me and for the gospel will save it" (Mark 8:35).

Everyone needs to be gripped by a deeply absorbing purpose that will give direction, power, and meaning to life. A meaningful life becomes possible when a person believes that activities and relationships are directly and vitally connected to goals. Ambition and responsible behavior result when these goals seem supremely worthwhile and attainable. For the Christian, the goal of living life to the glory of God is supremely worthwhile. Is this goal attainable? Get the answer yourself from the final words of the resurrected Christ as recorded in Matthew:

All authority in heaven and on earth has been given to me. Therefore go and make disciples

of all nations, baptizing them in the name of
the Father and of the Son and of the Holy
Spirit, and teaching them to obey everything
I have commanded you. And surely I am with
you always, to the very end of the age.

MATTHEW 28:18–20

When taken seriously, such truth reaches the heart and remarkable results can follow. One of the most inspiring examples of this can be found in the book *Through Gates of Splendor* by Elisabeth Elliot, in which she writes about her husband, Jim, and four other young men who wanted to take the gospel to the savage Auca Indians. Their offer of friendship was rejected, and the Aucas brutally killed all five of those courageous missionaries. But Elisabeth and her daughter, Rachel, would not give up and eventually succeeded in taking the gospel to the very ones who had murdered Jim and his friends. Later, while reading Jim's journal, Elisabeth came across a sentence he had written that eloquently expresses the message of this chapter: "He is no fool who gives what he cannot keep to gain what he cannot lose."

The Straight Road

A DROPOUT AT THIRTEEN! She did it, she said, "to concentrate completely on my goal." Few thirteen-year-olds are that certain about their future. "Even then, I knew exactly what I wanted," she said. Her goal? To sing in the opera.

To reach that coveted goal, Roberta Peters had to spend many hours in vocal studies. Three years passed and she was offered the leading role in a Broadway musical. The salary looked astronomical and the lure of Broadway danced before her eyes. But if she signed the contract, it would mean being away from her training for opera for a year or more.

Needing advice, sixteen-year-old Roberta went to her teacher. He counseled her this way: "You are good, Roberta, but you can be better. If you take this detour, you'll never know how far along the straight road you might have gone." She refused the shortcut and four years later made her Metropolitan Opera debut in Mozart's *Don Giovanni*.

Credit (or discredit) our present-day culture for its influence on strengthening the appeal of the shortcut. Ours has been called the push-button society. The emphasis is on speed, and our computer culture makes it hard to develop patience. The "itch of the instantaneous" is a disease that is reaching epidemic proportions.

*L*ife's most treasured gifts take time to possess. There is no shortcut to Christian character, personality, poise, skill, a trained mind, and cultured maturity. These gifts cannot be hurried.

Remember the Red Queen in *Through the Looking-Glass*? Rushing through the Looking-Glass Wonderland with Alice in hand, she kept crying out all the time, "Faster! Faster! Don't try to talk. Faster!" Maybe the Red Queen is symbolic of our time. We should try to catch our breath long enough to ask if all this activity indicates achievement. You wonder if a certain pilot was speaking for us when in answer to a passenger's question, "How are we doing?" he replied, "We're lost, but we're making good time!"

Some young people in this hurry-hurry age are tempted to rush into marriage and take short-cuts in education and job preparation; it is uncommon to consider the counsel of Roberta Peters's teacher: "If you take this detour [or shortcut], you'll never know how far along the straight road you might have gone."

"The straight road" has no geometrical significance; rather, it means the best direction to take to reach a worthwhile goal. More often than not, "the straight road" looks like "the long way around."

Life's most treasured gifts take time to possess. There is no shortcut to Christian character, personality, poise, skill, a trained mind, and cultured maturity. These gifts cannot be hurried.

Robert Frost expressed the importance of our choices and their effects on our future in "The Road Not Taken," a poem you probably read in one of your English classes.

> *Two roads diverged in a yellow wood,*
> *And sorry I could not travel both*
> *And be one traveler, long I stood*
> *And looked down one as far as I could*
> *To where it bent in the undergrowth*
> *Then took the other. . . .*

Oh, I kept the first for another day!
Yet knowing how way leads on to way,
I doubted if I should ever come back.
I shall be telling this with a sigh
Somewhere ages and ages hence;
Two roads diverged in a wood, and I—
I took the one less traveled by,
And that has made all the difference.

Savanarola, one of the great spiritual leaders in Florence, Italy, was hanged in 1498, but some of his thoughts continue to live, offering deep insight for anyone wanting to resist the temptation of the shortcut and take the straight road instead. You will be a fortunate tassel-mover if you choose to live according to the counsel he gave so many years ago: "Would you rise in the world?" he asked. "You must work while others amuse them-selves. Are you desirous of a reputation for courage? You must risk your life. Would you be strong morally and physically? You must resist temptation. All this is paying in advance. Observe the other side of the picture: the bad things are paid for afterwards."

The straight road is traveled by those who choose to pay in advance for life's best. Many people are not attracted to this road. But if you are willing to do today what most people aren't, you will be able to live tomorrow in a way that most people can't. You will experience the priceless realization that when facing choices you chose the straight road and it made all the difference.

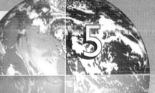

$\mathcal{O}$n
$\mathcal{M}$aking $\mathcal{D}$ecisions

SOME PEOPLE REMIND US of the

fellow who struggled with a bad case of

indecisiveness. He went to see a psychiatrist.

"So you have trouble making up your mind,"

said the doctor.

"Well, uh, uh," stammered the fellow, "well,

uh, yes and no."

Someone once asked J. L. Kraft, the great

manufacturer of cheese, to what he attributed

his success. "The ability to make up my mind,"

replied Kraft. He went on to explain his method:

"When I have a decision to make, first, I pray hard. Then I think hard, and when time is about up and I must have the answer, I say, 'Lord, now you show me the next thing to do.' Then the first idea that comes into my mind after I have gone through that process is what I take to be the answer. I have been correct a large enough percentage of the time to persuade me that this course is sound."

Notice the steps in Kraft's method: (1) earnest prayer: "I pray hard"; (2) deep thought: "I think hard"; (3) faith and action: "When time is about up and I must have the answer, I say, 'Lord, now you show me the next thing to do.' Then the first idea that comes into my mind . . . I take to be the answer."

Let's take those steps one at a time and examine them more closely. First, the matter of prayer. A great deal of soul-searching takes place in the senior year and after graduation. Important questions such as "Should I go to college?" "If so, where?" "Am I capable of succeeding in college?" "Should marriage come before choice of career or college?" "How will the economy affect my life?"—all these and more fill your mind.

So important are the answers to these questions! The wrong decision will seriously affect your future. How comforting in the face of these uncertainties are the words of Christ to every follower of his: "Ask and it will be given to you; seek and you will find; knock and the door will be opened to you" (Matt. 7:7).

His will for your life can be known, at least enough of it to guide you in deciding what to do next. It is unthinkable that the Christ of Calvary could want to show us his will less than we desire to know it!

The second step is "Think hard." Recall what you've learned from past experiences. Counsel with those who you think are best qualified to help you. Consider the alternatives to and the consequences of each choice.

Third, be determined to do what you think will enable you to travel in the direction of the kind of service for which Christ has given you special gifts. "Make level paths for your feet and take only ways that are firm" (Prov. 4:26).

The road that makes all the difference stretches out before you. John Oxenham, an English business-man and writer, called it the "high way" when he penned these familiar lines:

To every man there openeth
A way, and ways, and a way
And the High Soul climbs the High Way,
And the Low Soul gropes the Low.
And in between on the misty flats
The rest drift to and fro,
But to every man there openeth
A High Way and a Low.
And every man decideth
The way his soul shall go.

An impressive young man who wanted to take the "high way" to success walked up to Norman Vincent Peale—the famous author and minister—and said, "I've got a statement to make and a question to ask."

"Let's have them both," said Dr. Peale.

"First, I want a great future, and, second, I want to know how to make a good start," stated the young man.

Dr. Peale then asked, "And what kind of a future is that?" Some discussion followed as they worked toward a clearer understanding of what the young man really wanted to do with his life.

"Now," said Dr. Peale, "*when* do you want this great future to start?"

"Well," he replied, "sometime soon."

"That great future you want needs to start *now*," Dr. Peale challenged. He then shared with his young inquirer his famous ten-word formula for having a great future: "I can do all things through Christ who strengthens me" (Phil. 4:13 NKJV).

He urged the young man to place copies of this great verse all around him—on his bathroom mirror, in his car, on his desk. Dr. Peale assured him that with this powerful truth growing in his mind, he could be confident of having that great future.

You, too, can be confident of having that great future, by taking the "high way." You will need divine direction as you travel, and you can have it as you listen carefully: "Your ears will hear a voice behind you, saying, 'This is the way; walk in it' " (Isa. 30:21).

$\mathcal{C}$hoosing $\mathcal{Y}$our $\mathcal{W}$ork

YOU DON'T NEED TO BE REMINDED

that great care should be taken in choosing

your work. Nobody wants to be a vocational

misfit, and yet many people receive little or no

satisfaction from their jobs. For example, a

nationwide study conducted by the American

Institute of Public Opinion reveals that about

three out of every five workers feel that they

are wasting their time in jobs they dislike.

How can this mistake be avoided? Some

guidance regarding the problem was offered

by John Ruskin, who said: "In order that people may be happy in their work, these three things are needed: They must be fit for it; they must not do too much of it; and they must have a sense of success in it."

Let's focus on the first thing Ruskin mentions: "They must be fit for it." This kind of analysis is not easy. Matching a person with the work for which he or she is best suited requires an understanding of the person as well as the work. Often young people discover interests and abilities by taking vocational tests. These tests can rate your dexterity, your ability with numbers and words, and your sense of logic, insight, and judgment. Your state employment service can direct you to the proper places to take these tests. Also, you can take such tests at most colleges and universities.

For those who will be entering the work force immediately after graduation, a knowledge of job trends is valuable. You have graduated from high school at a time when the need for technical workers is becoming critical. Openings in this area include those for data-processing specialists, electronics technicians, technical secretaries, lab assistants, supervisors of production control, technical photographers, and government safety inspectors.

Usually there is a shortage of skilled workers: carpenters, bricklayers, plumbers, electricians, mechanics, lathe operators, and machinists.

A strong demand exists for sales and office workers: typists, secretaries, clerical workers, and retail and wholesale sales representatives.

When the time comes to seek employment,

you will need to be prepared for job interviews. Personnel directors responsible for interviewing young people who are looking for jobs seem to agree on certain basic points. Their advice includes:

1. Develop the fundamental skills of reading, writing, and arithmetic.

2. Dress appropriately when you go job hunting, and avoid the "take me for what I am, not for how I look" attitude. Remember you have only one chance to make a good first impression.

3. Show common courtesy. One personnel director of a large company who interviews dozens of young people every day complained of youthful applicants who chewed gum during interviews!

4. Go to the interview by yourself.

5. Display the "I really want to work" attitude.

6. Understand the principle of first things first. You don't need to ask about a pension plan in the first interview.

7. Answer all questions on the application. If you can't respond to a question, put a dash beside it so the personnel director will know you didn't overlook it.

8. Be on time. Punctuality reflects consideration for the personnel director and shows that you are a person with a sense of responsibility.

9. Write or print legibly. Carelessness in this matter wastes the personnel director's time.

Finally, remember to trust Christ to help you. He knows the anxieties of young job hunters. Having a sense of his presence will steady you.

$\mathscr{I}$s $\mathscr{C}$ollege for $\mathscr{M}$e?

FOLLOWING ARE SOME OF THE

questions most commonly asked by those

graduates who are wondering, "Is college

for me?"

Q. I'm trying to decide whether to go to

college. What information do I need to

help me make this decision?

A. When freshmen are asked why they

decided to go to college they typically

give the following answers:

To get a better job.
To acquire a general education.
To earn more money.
To please parents.
To get away from parents.
To meet interesting people.
To have something to do.

A significant number of young people entering college will drop out before graduation. Many studies have been made to determine why the dropout rate is so high. Researchers consistently discover that students often fail to make the connection between their purpose in life and education. Most young adults who drop out of college possess enough mental ability to succeed as college students. If they cannot relate their subjects and classroom work to present needs and future goals, however, the academic road

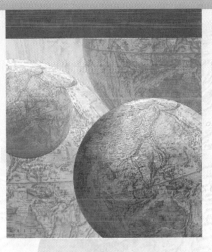

ABILITIES

With God's
guidance you
can find
training and
work that are
suited to your
abilities and
interests.

Abilities

Guidance

Interests

becomes too rough and appears to lead to no desired destination.

Other students have wrong motives for attending college and eventually drop out when their motives fail to carry them through. Some use college as a cop-out: "I'm going because there is nothing better to do," or "I'm going to escape for a while." Others see college as the royal route to success: "College will transform me into all I need to be to succeed." They view college as a cure-all, a guarantee of a secure future. Often these students are not willing to do the work necessary to succeed.

Those who do travel the college road often speak of experiencing greater personal growth, a sharper sense of purpose, and a higher development of skills. Any college worthy of the name should offer students the opportunities to discover and develop their abilities so that they can apply themselves at increasingly higher levels of performance to the glory of God.

Before you decide to attend college, examine your motives, realize you will need to keep your eye on your desired destination while also working through each step necessary to reach it, and though college should provide the proper environment and opportunities, the outcome of your college experience will depend on what you put into it.

Q. If going to college is presently out of the question, how can I further my education?

A. Correspondence courses are available.

Many of these courses can be taken for
college credit. For information write:

> National University Continuing
> Education Association
> One Dupont Circle, Suite 420
> Washington, D.C. 20036

More information can be obtained by ordering
the "Directory of Accredited Private Home
Study Schools" from:

> National Home Study Council
> 1601 18th Street
> Washington, D.C. 20009

Q. I've had my fill of school and formal
education. I'd like to do something with
my hands. Where can I get information
on job opportunities that offer training
programs and apprenticeships?

A. Contact the local branch office of your
   State Employment Security Commission
   to set up an appointment for aptitude
   testing and/or vocational counseling.
   That office will also have a listing of
   various job opportunities and apprenticeship programs available in your
   area of interest.

Employers in your city probably have an association that keeps an up-to-date listing of openings,
along with job descriptions and on-the-job training
opportunities.

Some corporations offer excellent trainee
programs that include aptitude testing and
apprenticeships in a wide variety of jobs.

Q. What are the alternatives for high school

graduates who are seeking to live meaningful, productive lives but who do not plan to go to college?

A. 1. Practical training is necessary to start a career. This "vocational" training is offered by trade schools and community colleges. Check your public library for resources on (a) kinds of jobs available, (b) where various kinds of work are performed, (c) what qualifications and training are needed, (d) salaries and working conditions, (e) obtainability of various jobs in the future, and (f) where further information is available.

2. Apprenticeship in a trade may be the route to a satisfying job. As an apprentice you would have a full-time job while you learn the skills of your trade.

3. Military service, with its advantages
   and disadvantages, is another alternative
   to college.

4. Other options include volunteer service,
   a year of traveling (if you have the
   finances!), and working to save money
   for specialized training in the future.

With God's guidance you can find training and
work that are suited to your abilities and interests.

$\mathscr{P}$ractical $\mathscr{Q}$uestions for the $\mathscr{C}$ollege $\mathscr{B}$ound

FOR THOSE WHO HAVE MOVED

one tassel and now aspire to move another,

the following questions and answers may offer

some guidance.

Q. How can I get information about

institutions of higher learning such as

Bible colleges and Christian liberal arts

colleges?

A. Many Christian graduates are attracted

to Bible colleges and Christian liberal

arts colleges, which offer a rich spiritual environment, high academic standards, highly qualified professors, and opportunities for meaningful service. For more information write:

> American Association of
>   Bible Colleges
> 130–F North College St.
> P.O. Box 1523
> Fayetteville, AR 72701

> Christianity Today, Inc.
> Creative Data Center
> 650 South Clark
> Chicago, IL 60605-9960

Q. How can I finance a college education?

A. Because of the soaring cost of attending college, an increasing number of students

need help financing their education.
Fortunately, a variety of loan programs
are available. Your high school guidance
counselor is one of the best sources for
information regarding these programs.
Ask for help. You'll be glad you did.

Additional sources of financial assistance can be found among the numerous state-level college assistance programs.

Scholarships may also be available to you. Check with your school or community library to acquaint yourself with commercially published scholarship guides. If you are physically handicapped or a child of a serviceman who was killed or permanently disabled in military action, benefit grants and other special financial aid are available.

The college of your choice probably has an employment service. If the college is located in a large city, employment may not be too difficult to find, but be sure to remember that school comes first!

Q. With college costs rising, I will need to work while I go to school. Are there programs that will help me earn money, choose a career, and impress future employers looking for talent, drive, and experience?

A. Yes, Co-op! Co-op (short for Coopera-tive Education) is a program linking the classroom with the workplace to provide an education with career relevance. Co-op gives students the opportunity to earn a regular paycheck and gain experience in a chosen career at the same time. The best guide to Co-op programs is the *Co-op Education Undergraduate Program Director,* which can be ordered from:

> National Commission for
>   Cooperative Education
> 350 Huntington Avenue
> Boston, MA 02115-5005

Q. What do admissions boards consider when admitting students to college?

A. 1. High school grade record.

2. Recommendation of the school principal or counselor.

3. College Board Scholastic Aptitude Test (SAT) scores.

4. Class standing.

5. School activities and positions held.

Personal qualities of prospective students are also important. Admissions officers are concerned about students' character, emotional stability, attitudes, and leadership qualities. Results of personal interviews are included in admission decisions at many colleges.

Good scholarship is to be desired, but it is the student's *total* record that will make the difference when applying to colleges.

Q. What are colleges expecting from today's high school graduates?

A. According to a report by the College Board, sponsor of the major college

entrance examination in the U.S., high
school graduates should be able to
write a "standard English sentence" and
"use effectively the mathematics of
algebra and geometry." They should also
know a foreign language and be able to
use computers. The report also empha-
sized the importance of the arts, claiming
that this dimension of education can
"challenge and extend the human
experience."

Q. Will a college education really increase
my earning power?

A. The evidence continues to support a
positive response to this question. An
economist for a life insurance company

estimated that for every dollar invested in a college education, the student gets at least twenty to thirty dollars in return.

L. H. Adolfson, of the University of Wisconsin, tells a story that contains excellent guidance for those who wonder if they should pursue more education. The story is about three horsemen of ancient times who were riding across a desert. As they crossed the dry bed of a river, out of the darkness a voice called, "Halt."

They obeyed. They were told to dismount, pick up a handful of pebbles, put the pebbles in their pockets, and remount.

After they had done as they were instructed, the voice said, "You have done as I commanded. Tomorrow at sunup you will be both glad and

SUCCEED

*A*verage students
who possess
strong ambition,
determination,
and a willingness
to work hard
can succeed
in college.

Willingness

Ambition

Determination

sorry." The three horsemen rode away thinking about the strange prediction.

The next morning at sunrise, they reached into their pockets and found that a miracle had happened. Instead of pebbles, they pulled out diamonds, rubies, and other precious stones. Then they saw the truth of the prophecy. They were both glad and sorry—glad they had taken some, and sorry they had not taken more.

And this, points out Dr. Adolfson, is the story of education.

Q. Can an average (C) student succeed in college?

A. High school graduates with a C average should not conclude that they are not smart enough to succeed in college. Of course, some colleges and universities are highly selective and competition is exceptionally difficult.

Average students are accepted by many good colleges and universities. Don't overlook the community college, for it can serve as an ideal training ground for testing your ability to succeed in college. Often in such a college you will receive greater personal attention from instructors. Many of these schools offer vocational programs that will help you develop marketable skills suitable to your style of life and community opportunities.

Average students who possess strong ambition, determination, and a willingness to work hard can succeed in college. Sometimes C students in high school become superior students in college!

Q. I'm having trouble getting accepted by a college. What should I do?

A. Start by contacting the following
    resources for assistance:

> American College Admissions
>   Advisory Center
> 2401 Pennsylvania Ave., Suite 1051
> Philadelphia, PA 19130
> Council of Independent Colleges
> One Dupont Circle N. W.,
> Suite 320
> Washington, D.C. 20036

For a small fee you can receive some excellent
information on how to find the right college or university, how to improve your chances for getting
accepted, and how to pay your way. Request the
"College Guide" from:

> Reprint Editor
> Reader's Digest
> Pleasantville, NY 10570

Q. After I decide on a college, then what?

A. 1. Obtain a catalog of the college or university you want to attend. You will be able to get it from the admissions officer at the college or in a library. Also obtain the catalog of the college of your second choice.

2. Use the catalogs to find out if you will be able to meet the academic standards required for admission.

3. Select two or three specific courses you think you might like to take and for which you will be able to meet the requirements. Do not make a final decision too hastily.

4. Note all dates with respect to enrollment, entrance, and scholarship examinations so that you will be able to complete all forms on time.

5. Make a budget for your first college
   year using the chart on the next page.

If you've decided college is for you, go for it!
Gather information, plan for the future, and be
willing to work hard. Your time, energy, and
resources will be well spent.

a. Tuition
   (see college catalog) $_____

b. Residence, if any
   (see catalog) $_____

c. Miscellaneous college
   expenses (see catalog) $_____

d. Books (see college
   catalog or visit the
   campus bookstore) $_____

e. Spending money
   (amount per week
   times 30 weeks) $_____

f. Money for emergencies
   (at least $200–$500) $_____

g. Transportation costs $_____

h. Clothes $_____

i. Other items such as possible
   medical and dental expenses,
   Christmas presents, etc. $_____

                    Total $_____

Yes, No, and Whoopee

GRADUATING SENIORS ARE MOVING

in the right direction if they're able to say yes,

no, and whoopee!

Let's start with the no. Today's tassel movers

are getting great amounts of advice empha-

sizing this powerful little word—no. Say no to

drugs. Say no to quick fixes and easy choices.

It's a vitally important word. If it's spoken at

the right time in the right situation in the right

way to the right person, it can give your heart

a song that will last for the rest of your life.

Failure to say no can strike a tragically different tune—addiction, loss of control, unwanted pregnancy, poor preparation, missed opportunity, and low self-esteem. There's very little joyous melody in a song we are forced to sing because we chose not to say no.

A prominent pastor shared his experience with a young man who came to him for counseling. The youth told his pastor that some friends had had a bad influence on his life. They enjoyed going to a particular club where they could get plenty of drugs, and he would go with them even though he had often promised himself and God that he would stop. He explained to his pastor that in spite of all his best intentions, he could not stop going with his friends and taking drugs. Now he was in the pastor's study hoping the pastor had an answer for him. And the pastor did indeed have an answer for him, but it was not the antidote the youth had expected. For the pastor simply said, "Son, why don't you stop?"

"I can't," he replied.

"What do you mean you can't stop?" asked the pastor. "You're the one who goes there. Nobody forces you. You're the one who takes the drugs. Nobody puts a gun to your head and makes you take them. So just stop."

"You know," replied the surprised youth, "nobody ever put it to me that way." Three weeks later the young man called his pastor and said, "You gave me the best advice I have ever received. You said stop and I did. I haven't touched drugs since I talked with you."

Choices! We *can* choose! We *can* change! We *can* choose to stop doing what is wrong, bad, foolish, and inappropriate. We *can* choose to start doing what is right, good, smart, and mature! Easy? No. Possible? Yes.

Freedom to choose means that I *can* let peer pressure control me. I *can* experiment with drugs and alcohol. I *can* compromise my moral standards. I *can* choose the quick, easy way. God gives us the freedom to choose. But when we exercise this freedom to choose, we must realize we are *not* free to control the consequence of our choices. Because we reap what we sow, we must understand where the problem starts and where it can lead. The following puts it in a nutshell:

Sow a thought, reap an act

Sow an act, reap a habit

Sow a habit, reap a character

Sow a character, reap a destiny

Saying a big
enough yes to
what is right,
good, and true
is the best way
to say no to
what is wrong,
bad, and false.

Serious drug addiction requires professional help. Christ-centered hospitalization programs are available. But before it gets that far, you do have a choice.

Saying no is important but not enough. Stopping what we ought to stop is necessary but falls short of an adequate answer. A simple story Jesus told long ago explains why. A man had an evil spirit that left him. Later it returned and found the "house" empty. So it went out and found seven other spirits more wicked than itself, and they all returned to the empty house and moved in. Tragically, the man's life became worse than before (see Matt. 12:43–45).

The lesson is clear. Sweeping the house clean by getting rid of what is bad is not enough. If we major in the negatives—what we *can't* do, where we *can't* go—our life's curriculum fails us. That is why Jesus told the story of the empty house. He wanted us to know that the power for living is in what we say yes to. Saying a big enough yes to what is right, good, and true is the best way to say no to what is wrong, bad, and false.

Say yes to the development of love, joy, peace, patience, kindness, goodness, faithfulness, gentleness, and self-control (see Gal. 5:22–23). These characteristics are admired by all sensible people, even those who don't believe in God. We are part of a "cut-flower generation." The virtues listed above are like flowers cut from their roots. These virtues are still found in our society but are severed from their living source—Christ. Like flowers no longer connected to life-giving roots and soil, these virtues sooner or later will wither and die. Our society's dilemma is the result of not knowing that all these virtues so highly valued by enlightened minds are spiritually connected to Christ, who said, "I am the way and the truth and the life" (John 14:6). To try to preserve what has been separated from the living source leads to the confusion and despair of our times.

Saying no and yes brings us to whoopee—the last part of our definition of the person growing in the right direction. Those who can say whoopee know how to *celebrate* life. Without ignoring life's trials, temptations, and difficult challenges, these fortunate individuals find special meaning in the common, ordinary things of life. Although they plan for the future and discipline themselves in the present, they enjoy the life they have

P
E
R
S
P
E
C
T
I
V
E

You can focus
on your strengths
and be aware of
your weaknesses.
You can keep
your perspective
without losing
sight of your
problems

now. Others enjoy being around them because this attitude is positively contagious.

Celebrating life is possible when life is meaningful, purposeful, and productive. The celebrative attitude allows for disappointment, failure, confusion, and mistreatment, and it rises above difficult, painful circumstances. When life rains on your parade, a celebrative approach keeps you optimistic without forcing you to deny that the rain is falling. You can focus on your strengths and be aware of your weaknesses. You can keep your perspective without losing sight of your problems. You can set realistic goals while experiencing a failure. You can learn to face the unfamiliar even as you feel afraid, insecure, or undeserving of success. You can seek help when you need it, knowing that sometimes life gets too big for any of us to handle alone. Sooner or later, the smartest, strongest, and bravest need others.

Your ability to celebrate life as you are called on to live it grows with the knowledge that God knows you, loves you, believes in you, and has allowed you to have your life. So live it to the fullest, because you not only have life, but as a Christian, you have a personal relationship with him who gave it.

This growing ability to say yes, no, and whoopee depends on our being able to experience the truth of one of Christ's most unforgettable statements: "I have come that they may have life, and have it to the full" (John 10:10).

As a graduate, you have moved the tassel and now possess a diploma—that special symbol of your accomplishment. If you continue to succeed in life by saying yes to what is right, no to what is wrong, and whoopee in celebration of the full life given to you in Christ, you are indeed to be congratulated.

With more than two million of his books in print, **Dr. Louis O. Caldwell** ranks as one of America's leading Christian authors. He received his doctorate in education with specialization in psychological counseling from the University of Houston. As president of Better Life Enterprises, International, Dr. Caldwell conducts seminars for singles, couples, men's groups, church leaders, and college students across the nation. A licensed marriage and family therapist, Dr. Caldwell is currently in private practice. He also serves as a consultant to Christian schools and colleges. He is a member of the American Association of Marriage and Family Therapists and a charter member of the American Association of Christian Counselors.